ACCOMMODATION

A TRAGICOMEDY

IN

ONE ACT

Melville Lovatt

TSL Drama

First published in Great Britain in 2017
By TSL Publications, Rickmansworth

Copyright © 2017 Melville Lovatt

ISBN / 978-1-911070-56-6

Image courtesy of :
https://openclipart.org/detail/191171/gents-play-cards

Rights of performance

Dedication

for
Peter Shimmin

By Melville Lovatt

Full Length Plays

Small Mercies	Comedy-Drama	4M	2F
The Powers That Be	Thriller	3M	3F + 1 boy
Visiting Time	Family Drama	3M	2F
Desperate Measures	Dark Comedy	3M	1F

One Act Plays

Accommodation	Tragicomedy	4M	1F
The Lamp	Comedy-Drama	1M	1F
The Distressed Table	Comedy-Drama	1M	1F + Voiceover (F)
The Boomerang	Comedy-Drama	3M	1Boy + Voiceover (F)
The Kiss	Thriller	2M	1F
The Weekend	Drama	2M	1F
The Grave	Drama	2M	

Monologue Collections

Standing Alone (16 monologues)	Comedy-Drama	8M	8F

All enquiries to TSL Publications: www.tslbooks.uk

Accommodation

was first presented by
Forestage Theatre Company

on
23 March 1976

at
The Little Theatre,
Upper St Martin's Lane, London

with the following cast:

George Dixon	**Peter C. Read**
Brenda Dixon	**Phyllis Ferguson**
Derek	**Robert Champion**
Don	**Alan Cody**
Tony	**Stephen Riddle**

Director:
Kendall Johns

The production was supported
by
The Arts Council Of Great Britain

Characters

GEORGE DIXON: *a man in his early fifties.*

BRENDA DIXON: *a woman in her mid forties.*

DEREK: *a man of twenty-five.*

DON: *a man of twenty-eight.*

TONY: *a man of twenty-one.*

Running Time 65 mins

1970. Winter. Evening.

The chart topper, 'Groovin' With Mr Bloe' blares out loudly.

The dining-room/lounge of a rooming house in South East London. The room is large, extending the width of the stage.

CL wall, a door.

UL slightly from door, a small dining-table with four matching chairs.

CR wall, a mantelpiece with chiming clock. An electric fire.

DR, a small television.

SC, 3 seat settee with one matching armchair.

The room, through a window, suggested, upfront, overlooks the garden.

The overall impression is utilitarian, slightly shabby.

Music fades out.

DON, DEREK and **TONY**

TONY *is sitting at the table, eating slowly, clearly not enjoying his meal. He sports longish hair and is trendily dressed.*

DON *sits in the armchair, staring solemnly up at the ceiling. He is plainly, conservatively dressed.*

DEREK sits on the settee, reading a newspaper. He wears faded denim jeans with matching top.

       Silence.

       TONY finds he can't eat his food, pushes plate away in disgust.

TONY: Usual crappy meal to round off the day.

       (Points to plate.) These runner beans are as hard as a rock.
       And as for the meat … I wouldn't give it to a dog.
       This place is the pits. It's gotta be the pits.
       (Stands.)
       Bloody prison food's better than *this*.
       (Pause.)
       TONY saunters over to DON.

       Can I cadge a fag?

DON: Sure.

TONY: Do you mind?

DON: *(Gives him cigarette.)* No, I've plenty.

TONY: *(Lights up.)* Left mine at work.

DEREK: *(Without looking up.)* Again?

TONY: Straight up.

DEREK: Third time this week.

TONY: *(To DON.)* I'll push you one back.

       (Pause.)

DEREK: *(Suddenly giggles.)* Here, seen this?

DON: What's that?

DEREK: Kaw, what a laugh. *(Reads aloud from newspaper.)* Milly insisted in Court that she only slept in Trafalgar Square to keep the pigeons company.

DON: *(Chuckles.)* No. Getaway.

TONY: *(Grins.)* It don't say that.

DEREK: *(Tosses newspaper to DON.)* Never a dull moment is there.

TONY: *(To DEREK, as DON reads.)* Did you read that last week?

DEREK: Eh?

TONY: *(Sits on settee arm.)* Some old geezer ... *(Small chuckle.)* got nicked having it away on a park bench.

DEREK: Oh?

TONY: In broad daylight too. It was in *The Evening News.* Eighty-eight he was.

DEREK: *(Grins.)* Nah I'm not having that.

TONY: No kidding.

DEREK: How old was the girl?

TONY: Only eighteen.

DEREK: Stroll on.

TONY: Just shows...

DEREK: The older the fiddle the better the tune.

TONY: Eighty-eight.

DEREK: So what happened?

TONY: Happened?

DEREK: In Court?

TONY: Well, the Judge was in two minds. Couldn't quite decide whether to award the pair of 'em medals for bravery or fine them both for indecency instead.

DEREK: What did he do?

TONY: Fined them fifty quid.

DEREK: Expensive shag.

TONY: That's what the old boy said.

(Pause.)

DON: *(Giggles, tosses newspaper onto settee.)* Never a dull moment.

DEREK: Hilarious ain't it?

DON: Bet they pissed their sides.

DEREK: It's original.

DON: You know who it is?

DEREK: Who?

DON: That old dear we've seen walking up and down the Edgware Road.

DEREK: Oh *her.*

DON: I bet it's her, alright. She's called Milly.

DEREK: Always wheeling a pram?

DON: That's right. Full of all sorts of rubbish.

DEREK: She stinks something awful.

DON: She's been on the road years.

TONY: *(Sits on settee arm, between DEREK and DON.)* Y'know I had a chat with her once. On Edgware Road. Just happened to be passing ... her pram had toppled over ... so I stopped to help her pick all her rubbish up. She's a highly intelligent woman. Holds a Degree in Philosophy. Least, I think it's Philosophy. Philosophy or Psychology. One or the other. Just forget which.

DON: Really?

TONY: She's all there with her mint drops. Enlightened me on several points of reference. Apparently, I was the first person she'd spoken to for over six weeks.

DON: That so?

TONY: Yeah. I was glad I'd stopped to help her.

Found her very interesting. *(Gets up, stands.)* It was a stimulating conversation altogether, really.

The only trouble was ... she became ... obstreperous.

Became far too pushy trying to cadge a fag off me.

I mean, I wouldn't have minded normally. I'd have given her one gladly. But it was a Thursday and I was skint. Stony broke.

Only had three fags to last me all night.

(Pause.)

Well, she wouldn't accept this. Began demanding to search me.

Demanding to search me. How hard faced can you get?

I mean, I'd only stopped to help her out of the goodness of my heart. I didn't *have* to stop. Could have carried on walking.

Ignored her completely. No skin off my nose.

But I stop to help her and the next thing is she starts playing on my good nature. Well ...

DEREK: So what did you do?

TONY: *(Rises.)* Well, what could I do? She starts tugging on my jacket.

Going hysterical. Shouting and screaming all kinds of abuse.

(Pause. He moves to table.)

So anyway, to cut a long story short, I let fly with two quick jabs to her ribcage, put the boot in a couple of times to her rear, sat her in the pram and kind of left it like that.

(Pours milk into cup.) Worked off the sweat in a pub around the corner. *(To DON, sits at table.)* Seeing your girl tonight?

DON: *(Rather sadly.)* No ... not tonight.

DEREK: *(Makes thumbs down sign.)* Hello.

DON: I phoned her up ... I was all set to go.

Well, she said her youngest son was ill.

Last week it was her eldest.

DEREK: So you're not going?

DON: No.

(Pause.)

Looks like it's on the scrap heap.

DEREK: How d'you mean?

DON: *(Wearily.)* Had a bit of a row. She hung up on me.

It was nothing, really. Storm in a teacup.

(Pause.)

She asked would I mind if we gave it a miss.

I said, no, I wouldn't mind, providing her youngest son really was ill.

(Short ironical laugh.)

Well, she asked me what that was supposed to mean so I told her what I was beginning to think and after a brief but very loud skirmish she slammed the phone down and that was that.

DEREK: Uh. Just like that, eh?

DON: Just like that. To hell with her anyway. She can jump in the lake.

I've reached a stage now where I just can't be bothered.

Honestly, Derek, it's not worth all the trouble.

I've fallen over backwards to please this girl and what thanks do I get? She treats me like shit. Well, I'm tired of groping around for the answers. There's no pleasing women.

I'm convinced of that. I've come to the conclusion that you just can't be right. Not with women, anyway. I've come to this conclusion.

TONY: Y'gotta treat 'em rough, mate. There's no other way.

They respect you more. No two ways about it.

If they think you're sensitive they'll kick you in the balls.

Walk all over you if you give 'em half a chance.

DEREK: Too true they will.

TONY: *(To DON.)* I used to be like you. Far too sensitive for my own good.

Still am for that matter. Far too sensitive. But I got wise, y'see.

I don't let it show. I came to terms with it. Turned it to my advantage.

DEREK: *(To DON.)* You're better off without her. She's pissing you about.

DON: She clearly thinks I'm soft in the head.

TONY: *(To DON.)* That's what you get when they know you're sensitive.

DON: Oh , I couldn't give a toss now.

DEREK: You'd go round the bend.

DON: If she writes I won't answer.

DEREK: There'd be no point.

DON: Exactly.

(Pause.)

DEREK: Do you think she will write?

DON: I'm certain she will. I left fifteen quid on the dressing table.

DEREK: Oh ... well, she'll send that back, then.

DON: With a cryptic note.

DEREK: She might just send the money.

DON: I just couldn't care less.

TONY: *(Saunters to DON.)* Come out with me tomorrow night.

I'll find you a bird in no time at all.

Took a bloke from work along with me the other week.

He was pissed off. Just finished with his bird.

Well, she'd finished with him but that's beside the point.

I took this bloke along with me. Went up The Empire.

In no time at all I'd got him fixed up. Y'see I know 'em all there.

Well, the ones I don't know are not worth bothering with.

Take it from me.

(Pause.)

The birds I don't know are either sweet sixteens and never been kissed, or over the hill, pushing fifty, been shagged, bagged and quartered by all and gentry.

DEREK: What's wrong with sweet sixteens?

TONY: *(Dismissive.)* You can keep 'em for yourself.

(Sits on chair arm.) No, give me a woman with a bit of experience.

(Pause.)

I'll never forget picking up a girl there once.

She was sixteen ... well, just turned seventeen.

I thought I'd have a change. Take a younger bird out.

(Pause.)

Danced with her all night. Not a bad looking bint.

Had her father's car parked outside.

Took me for a spin around Hampstead Heath.

(Pause.)

Thought I was well away. Bob's your uncle.

She parks the car in a nice secluded spot.

Ideal spot it was. Highly romantic. I thought, cracked it here, boy.

(Pause.)

But it wasn't so easy.

(Pause.)

There I was, just getting down to it. Taking the necessary safety precautions, when she tells me, completely out of the blue, that she's changed her mind. She doesn't want to do it.

Says she's seriously thinking of becoming a nun.

DEREK: Getaway.

TONY:. *(Stands.)* Straight up. I was absolutely speechless!

(Pause.)

Anyway, I said, you're gonna *have* to do it.

Whether you intend becoming a bloody nun or not.

What do you take me for? A Buddhist monk or something?

DON: So you took her by force?

TONY: She went berserk on me. Threw a canary fit. Fought all the way.

I got home, found she'd scratched my back something awful.

(Shakes head regretfully.) Never again, boy. Never again.

DEREK: It's better when they struggle.

TONY: Think so?

DEREK: More fun.

TONY: *(Sits next to DEREK.)* No, give *me* a woman with a bit of experience.

(Long Pause.)

DON: Anything on telly?

DEREK: Dunno. Switch it on.

DON: *(Glancing at watch.)* No, it's too early.

DEREK: There's a film on at seven.

DON: Film?

DEREK: Yeah. On B.B.C. Laurence Harvey's in it.

DON: What is it?

DEREK: Just forget …

DON: Butterfield Eight?

DEREK: On the tip of my tongue …

DON: Room At The Top?

DEREK: No, it ain't that. *(Picks up newspaper.)* Let's have a look.

DON: Second page, I think.

DEREK: Here we are.

DON:	What is it?
DEREK:	Walk On The Wild Side.
TONY:	*(Groans.)* Walk On The Wild Side. Seen it umpteen times.
DON:	*(To DEREK.)* Do you want to watch it?
DEREK:	*(Indifferently.)* Switch it on if you like.
DON:	No, I'm not really bothered. I've seen it as well.
	(He sits next to DEREK.
	Long Pause.)
	Y'know something?
DEREK:	What?
DON:	There's only us here.
DEREK:	How come?
DON:	All the rest are away.
DEREK:	Away?
DON:	On holiday. They've all gone home.
	(Pause.)
DEREK:	What about Frank?
DON:	He left this morning.
DEREK:	Never says much, does he?
DON:	No, he's very quiet.
DEREK:	Cagey.
DON:	Very cagey.
DEREK:	Funny bloke altogether, really.
TONY:	You two out tonight?
DEREK:	Might go out later on.
DON:	Me too.
DEREK:	*(To DON.)* Around ten?
DON:	Try a couple of halves.

DEREK:	That's all I can afford.
TONY:	Well, look, if this bird phones me up whilst I'm out –
DEREK:	You going out *again?*
TONY:	Gotta go to the doctor's.
DEREK:	What's wrong with you *this* time?
TONY:	*(Grimaces, rubs chest.)* My heart.
DEREK:	*(Laughs.)* Nah!
TONY:	No kidding….
DEREK:	*(Mockingly, to DON.)* Heart trouble.
DON:	*(Laughs.)* At his age.
DEREK:	*(Laughs.)* Jesus. *(Leans his face close to TONY'S.)* We invited to the funeral?
TONY:	*(Irritated, rises quickly.)* Piss off.
DEREK:	*(Grins, shakes head.)* Stroll on.
TONY:	Now look, if this bird phones me up whilst I'm out, tell her I've moved … done a moonlight or something. Just say I've moved to another address. If she asks where … tell her you haven't the foggiest. Okay?
DEREK:	Yeah, but listen –
TONY:	She'll probably phone around nine.
	I've been trying to get her off my back for weeks.
	She keeps on pestering me. Phoning me up.
DON:	So what does she want?
TONY:	Oh it's a bloody long story.
	(Pause.)
	I met her at a party a few months ago.
	I'd had a few drinks. Been on gin all night.
	Well, no, not all night. I started on beer.

Anyway, the thing was I'd arrived there too late.

All the best birds were taken. I was scraping the barrel.

Could have found better talent in an old folks' home.

(Pause.)

I'm stood at the bar. Just about to leave.

When, Bob's your uncle, I happen to glance round and this tart's stood next to me waiting to order me a drink.

(Pause.)

Now true enough, she was no raving beauty.

(Remembering.) To be honest, she was no beauty at all.

But I thought, what the hell. Anything's better than nothing.

You don't look at the mantelpiece when you're poking the fire.

(Pause.)

So I bought her a drink. One or two drinks.

We exhausted numerous topics of conversation then she invited me back to her place for coffee.

(Pause.)

By this time I was pissed out of my mind.

(Pause.)

When we got to her place I collapsed on the bed.

I remember, quite clearly, collapsing, fully clothed.

(Pause.)

The only other thing I remember is having a shocking dream.

Shocking. Dreamt I was eating a giant marshmallow.

Woke up. Couldn't find the pillow anywhere.

The silly cow had hidden it. Hidden it under the bed.

(As DIXON enters, holding a tray.)

She'd also stripped me down bollock naked.

(DIXON stands, watching TONY.)

TONY: *(His back to DIXON, unaware of his presence.)*

Well, anyway, the upshot of all this is … the reason she keeps phoning … keep it to yourselves … is that she insists I've made her pregnant. Put her in the pudding club.

How ridiculous can you get? I mean, it's out of the question.

I never got round to it. I was too busy eating this giant marshmallow!

DEREK: Leave it with us, then. A fiver? Alright?

TONY: A fiver?

DEREK: It's *got* to be worth a few drinks.

DIXON: *(To TONY, moves towards table.)* I don't want her round here.

Do you here me? That clear? *(Puts plates on tray.)* I don't want no scrubbers banging on my front door.

TONY: *(Turns to DIXON.)* Oh c'mon, you're only jealous.

DIXON: Just keep her away from here, that's all.

(Pause.)

That's all I need. Pregnant tarts at my door.

Pregnant scrubbers banging away on my front door.

(Pause.)

That's all I need.

(Pause.)

Just keep her away.

(Pause.)

Do you hear me?

TONY: *(Going off.)* I hear you. *(To DON and DEREK.)* See you later.

DON: Righto.

DEREK: Leave it with us.

(TONY goes out, closing the door.

Silence.

DIXON begins folding the tablecloth.

DON and DEREK sit.

DIXON turns to them.)

DIXON: Not that I wasn't a bit of a lad, myself.

I was. Don't mind admitting it.

(Pause.)

Don't let it fool you. I've been around too.

(Sits on settee arm.) But the difference is ... between me and him ... is that *I* never inconvenienced other people.

(Pause.)

If I made any mess, I cleaned it up myself.

(Pause.)

 Not like him.

(Pause.)

I've seen his type before.

DEREK: *(Stands, to DIXON.)* I can see you've been around.

(Standing over DIXON.) Been a tearaway in your time.

(To DON.) No doubt about it. You can see it in his eyes.

His nose. His ears. His overall physique.

You can tell he's been around. Stands out a mile.

His stance. His speech. His articulate expression.

(BRENDA appears, stands, arms folded, in doorway.)

DIXON: *(Unaware of BRENDA.)* I've played the field.

Don't mind admitting it. Before I got married.

Sowed a few wild oats.

(Pause.)

Talk about women? Talk to *me* about women?

(Points towards doorway, without turning to it.) I've been through more women than he's been through Shredded Wheat.

(Pause.)

I remember once ... this is no exaggeration ... I had a different woman every night of the week for just over six months.

Six months. Non stop.

DEREK: *(Leaning over DIXON.)* Six months?

DON: *(Gets up.)* Non stop?

DEREK: Without taking a breather?

DON: *(Stands over DIXON.)* How did you manage that?

DIXON: *(Shrugs.)* Just a question of stamina. I had plenty stamina.

Never used to drink or smoke. Kept myself fit. As simple as that.

(Pause.)

No, it wasn't *just* that. I had this knack ... of ...
well ... in those days I could *pace* my performance.

DEREK: Really?

DIXON: I could control my technique. Avoid wearing myself
out on any one woman.

DEREK: It's a pity you never wrote a book on the subject.

Outlined your technique in a illustrated manual.

Imagine! George Dixon. Sexologist. I can see it
now.

The definitive work. Worldwide bestseller. All sex
problems solved.

They'd be *queuing* to buy it.

DIXON: *(Seriously, thoughtful.)* Do you think so?

DEREK: *Right.* You've missed your way, mate. *No* mistake.

You're in the wrong business. *(Sighs, shakes head.)*
What a waste.

(Turns to DON.) What a waste, Don.

DON: Yeah. He's missed his way.

DEREK: Could have made a fortune.

(Suddenly excited.) Here, it's still not too late.

I'll get in touch with Playboy Magazine!

DIXON: *(Worriedly.)* Here, now hang on a minute ...

DON: Arrange a meeting.

DEREK: Exclusive interview.

DON: Boost their sales.

DEREK: *(Leans over DIXON.)* They'll make you a doctor.

DON: *(Does likewise.)* An alderman.

DEREK: Flock to you.

DON: From far afield.

DEREK: South Shields.

DON: Manchester.

DEREK: Ramsbottom.

DON: Stockport.

BRENDA: STOP IT!

(Silence.

All three turn, stare at BRENDA.

DIXON rises to his feet.

BRENDA moves, slowly, towards him.

She stands, arms folded.)

DIXON: *(Apologetically, to BRENDA.)* Look … *(Breaks off.)*

(Pause.)

DEREK: *(To DON.)* Fancy a game of darts?

DON: *(Nods.)* Wouldn't say no.

(DEREK exits, followed by DON.

Silence.

DIXON turns away, starts to mutter.)

DIXON: Ignorant bastards. That's all they are, the pair of 'em.

BRENDA: What do you expect? Just what do you expect?

So you could *pace* your performance, could you?

All a question of stamina?

(As DIXON turns away from her, moves towards window.)

As simple as that?

DIXON: *(Softly.)* I was only joking.

BRENDA: I'll say you were joking. *(Sharp.)* You'd *have* to be joking.

Wouldn't you?

(Pause.

BRENDA picks up newspaper, sits in the armchair.
She tosses newspaper onto settee.
She sighs, stares ahead.
DIXON stands, looking out, his back to her.
Silence.)

DIXON: *(Quietly.)* Looks like rain. Think we're in for a storm.
(Pause.)
S'funny. Always rains on Wednesday.
(Pause.)
These last five weeks. Five or six weeks.
(Pause.)
I've noticed. Every Wednesday without fail. Always rains.
(Silence.
DIXON stares out.)

BRENDA: *(Looks at DIXON.)* Did you get all the rent?
(DIXON nods, without turning.)
No trouble?

DIXON: *(Softly.)* No.
(Pause.)

BRENDA: What about the Irishman? Whatsisname ...?

DIXON: *(Turns to face her.)* Who?

BRENDA: Jennings?

DIXON: He paid.

BRENDA: Two weeks.

DIXON: *(Nods, turns back to window.)* Paid up.
(Pause.)

BRENDA: Did Martindale pay?

DIXON: *(Wearily.)* Yes.

BRENDA:	Have to watch *him*.
DIXON:	I know.
BRENDA:	He'll do us.
DIXON:	I'll watch him.
BRENDA:	When's he come back?
DIXON:	Saturday.
BRENDA:	*(Pondering.)* Mmn …

(Pause.)

Don't trust him. Needs watching. Where's he from? Up north?

(Pause.)

Leaves his room like a pigsty. Every single morning.

DIXON: *(Wearily.)* I've told him about it.

BRENDA: *(Sharp.)* Well, tell him again.

(Pause.)

More trouble than he's worth. His room's like a tip. Stinks to high heaven. What's he smoking in there?

(Pause.)

I *dread* going in. Have to spray the room out. Every morning. Smells terrible. Have to open the windows and spray the room.

(Pause.)

He's smoking something … pot or something. Smells worse than a thousand farts!

(Pause.)

DIXON: *(Wearily.)* I could give him the boot. Have *another* room empty?

(Turns to her.) Is that what you want?

Shall I give him the boot?

(Pause.)

BRENDA: *(Irritated, after considering.)* Warn him. Just give him one last warning. He wouldn't be tolerated anywhere else.

He'd be out on his ear the first week. *No* messing.

We're too soft, that's our trouble. Too bloody soft.

(Sighs wearily, shakes head.) Why's it always have to be us who gets lumbered?

(DIXON picks up the tray.)

Always has to be us. One mess after another.

(As DIXON turns away towards door.) It's beyond me why you took him on in the first place. You could *see* what he is.

DIXON: *(Faces her, puts down tray on table.)* How do you mean?

BRENDA: You could see he isn't clean.

DIXON: Beyond you? *Listen* –

BRENDA: We're not *that* hard up, are we? Well, *are* we?

DIXON: *(Jabs at her with forefinger.)* Listen, *you* said …!

(He breaks off impatiently, picks up tray, storms out.)

BRENDA: *(Shouts after him.)* Are we? We're not that hard up, surely!

(Silence.

BRENDA stands, shaking her head.

She picks up newspaper, sits on settee.

She kicks off her slippers, lies full-length.

She flicks through the pages.

Silence.

DIXON re-enters, stands by the door.

He stares at BRENDA.

Silence.)

DIXON: *(Quietly.)* I was thinking we could … go out somewhere tonight.

BRENDA: *(Dully.)* Out?

DIXON: *(Moves nearer to her.)* For a meal or something.

It'd make a change. Could go up the West End.

(Pause.)

Could try that new place. What's it called?

Y'know … the Italian place you were talking about last week?

(Pause.)

Could go there if you like.

(Pause.)

We don't *have* to have a meal.

Could just go for a drink. Try a couple at the Raven.

They've modernised it, now. I was in there last week.

Different place altogether. Fitted carpets. The lot.

A new landlord too.

(Pause.)

Seems a nice enough bloke. Easy going. Cheerful.

Gone down well with the locals. I've never seen it so packed.

(Pause.)

The beer's improved too.

(Pause.)

He's right on the ball.

(Pause.)

Knows how to *keep* beer.

(Pause.)

Takes a pride in his pint.

(Pause.)

(Turns to her.) Well, what do you say?

Could go out for an hour. It'd make a change.

You'd like it there now.

(Silence.

BRENDA stares at newspaper.

DIXON stares at her a moment, moves away to window.

He stands, looking out, hands on hips.

Silence.)

(Quietly.) I see old Andrew's got himself a new lawnmower.

(Pause.)

About time he got one. High time he did.

(Pause.)

Begrudges spending anything. That's *his* trouble.

(Pause.)

Bit of a miser. Think that's what it is.

(Pause.)

Think that's what it is. He don't like to spend.

(Pause.)

Bit of a skinflint. Bit of a Scrooge.

(Pause.)

Can't be badly off. His dad left him plenty.

(Pause.)

Can't be badly off. Not short of a few bob.

(Pause.)

(Turns to her.) I mean, you'd think he'd spend a ... bit on ... comforts.

You'd think he'd make life easier ... for himself.

(Turns back to the window.)

But he don't. Never spends. Never spends a far-thing.

(Pause.)

His old man was the same.

(Pause.)

(Softly, closing eyes.) Like father ... like ... *(Breaks off.)*

(Silence.)

BRENDA   *(Softly, turning to look at DIXON.)* I don't ... really feel like ... going out tonight.

(DIXON turns, looks at her.)

I don't feel like ... going for a meal or a drink.

(Pause.)

I don't really want ... I don't really feel ... I just feel like ... staying in ... like we used to ... staying in and ... *(Impatient, slams down newspaper, lies back, stares at ceiling.)* Staying in.

(Silence.

DIXON stares at BRENDA, turns slowly back to the window.

Silence.

BRENDA picks up her slippers, rising to her feet.

She stares at DIXON, moves towards him, stops.

She shakes her head, turns, goes out.

Silence.

DIXON turns, stares after BRENDA a moment.

He moves, slowly, to the armchair.

Silence.

He sits, slumped, gazing straight ahead.

He gazes, slowly, up at the ceiling, begins to sob, quietly, head in hands.

Fade.

Lights up.

DEREK and DON entering as the clock strikes 12. Midnight.)

DEREK: *(Rubs hands together, entering first.)* Bit chilly in here.

                Bloody freezing. *(Moving towards fire.)* Turn the fire on a minute.

DON: It's not working.

DEREK: No! Ain't he fixed it *yet?*

DON: Nope.

DEREK: Well why not?

DON: *(Shrugs.)* Don't ask me.

DEREK: *(Points to fire.)* It's been like that three weeks.

DON: I've told him about it.

DEREK: *Everybody's* told him. He couldn't give a shit.

                (DON sits in armchair.)

                We could freeze to death. He wouldn't bat an eyelid.

                My room's like an iceberg as well. Guess what?

                I woke up this morning. Put my underpants on.

                Guess what's in them? Icicles. *Icicles.*

DON: *(Grins, disbelievingly.)* Nah.

DEREK: No kidding. Icicles.

DON:	Icicles?
DEREK:	*Icicles.*
DON:	You're pulling my pisser.
DEREK:	I'll show that to you if you like.
DON:	*(Quickly.)* I believe you.
DEREK:	They've *still* not thawed out.
DON:	*(Disbelievingly.)* Getaway.
DEREK:	Sick and tired of it, I am.
DON:	Well, at least you've a heater.
DEREK:	A what?
DON:	A heater. There's none in my room.
DEREK:	A heater you call it? Do me a favour.
	I could get more heat lighting one of your farts.
DON:	Look, there's far worse places ...
DEREK:	I can't think of any.
DON:	Oh come on, it's not so bad.
DEREK:	*(Flops down on settee.)* Toss us a fag.
	(Pause.
	DON tosses a cigarette to DEREK.
	They both light up.
	Pause.)
	Y'know something?
DON:	What?
DEREK:	I'm thinking of emigrating.
DON:	Emigrating? Where?
DEREK:	*(Shrugs.)* God knows.
DON:	Uh. Thought about it, myself.
DEREK:	You've nothing to lose.

DON:	This country's buggered.
DEREK:	Needs a revolution.
DON:	An earthquake.
DEREK:	A hurricane. A kick up the arse.

DEREK: *(Pause.)*

Where would you emigrate?

DON: Australia.

DEREK: *(Grimaces.)* Australia?

DON: What's wrong with Australia?

DEREK: *(Shakes head.)* Set of bloody convicts. I mean, *every* bugger's on the fiddle out there.

DON: Thought you'd finished with crime.

DEREK: Can't afford to go straight.

DON: They'll have you.

DEREK: Look, I've been thinking …

DON: What?

DEREK: *(Softer, leans closer to DON.)* This jeweller's round the corner …

DON: Forget it.

DEREK: Listen –

DON: Count me out.

DEREK: Piece of cake.

DON: *(Unimpressed.)* Oh *really?*

DEREK: *It is.* I just go in the back … all you do is keep a look-out …

DON: Look, it's not my line, mate.

DEREK: Not your line? What *is* your line? Doughnuts? Making doughnuts?

DON: Listen –

DEREK: *(Scoffs.)* Is that your line? Doughnuts?

DON: Piss off.

DEREK: *(Chuckles.)* Stroll on.

DON: Look, I don't mind a … *(Breaks Off.)*

DEREK: What?

DON: A *legitimate* fraud, but –

DEREK: Legitimate fraud?

DON: *(Impatient.)* You know what I mean.

DEREK: No, I don't. Explain.

DON: I take after my old dad.

We've never believed in *breaking* the law.

But *bending* it? Well, that's a different thing.

Years ago, dad put an ad in the local paper.

Cup Final Seats For Sale. Five Pounds.

DEREK: Cup Final seats?

DON: *Seats.* Get it? When someone sent him a fiver for a seat, he'd send 'em a seat. A small stool he'd knocked together himself.

DEREK: *(Grins.)* I like it!

DON: Y'see? A *legitimate* fraud.

DEREK: *(Enthusiastically.)* Think I'll try that myself.

DON: *(Frowns.)* Oh they'd catch you today.

DEREK: How come?

DON: Trades Descriptions Act.

DEREK: Shit.

DON: But that's more *my* line.

DEREK: I'm doing the jeweller's. I'm doing the jeweller's.

You coming in or not?

(Door heard banging, below.

They stand, listening.)

TONY'S Voice, Off: *(Singing rather drunkenly.)* Weeeeeeee'll drink a drink a drink to Lilly The Pink A Pink A Pink

(Louder, combining with clumping footsteps.)

The saviour of the human ra-----aa-----aaace!

DON: *(Groans, looks towards door.)* God help us.

TONY'S Voice, Off: She invented Medicinal Compound

Now they call 'errrrrrrr ...

(Singing ends abruptly as someone is heard falling

with a loud crash outside the door.

Loud groaning heard, off.

DON moves quickly to the door.

DEREK, irritated, follows.

They exit.

More groaning, commotion heard, off.

They re-enter, carrying TONY.)

DON: *(To TONY, as TONY groans.)* C'mon, you'll be alright.

DEREK: Met with a bang.

TONY: *(Clutching head, in agony.)* Broke my bloody ankle, I'm sure.

DON: Which one?

TONY: *(Whimpering, as they drop him onto settee.)* Oh shit.

DEREK: Which ankle is it?

TONY: THOSE FUCKING STAIRS!

DON: Shush!

TONY: *(Grimaces.)* Shit.

DON: *(Worriedly.)* You'll have Dixon down on us.

DEREK:	*(Impatient.)* Which ankle, Tony?
TONY:	*(Hysterical with pain.)* My right! My right!
DON:	Quiet. Keep it down.
TONY:	Keep it down, he says!
DON:	You'll wake all the street up.
TONY:	*(Clutches head in agony.)* Oh God.
DEREK:	*(Attempts to remove TONY'S shoe.)* C'mon, let's have a look.
TONY:	Don't touch it!
DON:	Shush!
DEREK:	*(Softly.)* Alright. Lie still.
DON:	*(Softly.)* Take it easy.
DEREK:	Relax.
DON:	It's only a sprain.
TONY:	*(Grimaces, shakes head.)* I heard something crack.
DON:	Surprised Dixon's not down by now.
DEREK:	He will be in a minute
DON:	*(To TONY.)* You're as white as a sheet.
TONY:	*(Gasps for breath.)* Got a mouth like the desert.
DON:	Look like death warmed up.
TONY:	Alright! Don't rub it in!
DON:	*(Sniffing TONY.)* You been drinking whisky?
DEREK:	*(Sniffing TONY.)* Yeah, I can smell whisky
DON:	Never touch it, myself. It affects my breathing. Makes me fart all night.
DON:	Gives *me* diarrhoea.
DEREK:	*Very* bad for the guts. Corrodes the liver. It polished off my uncle.
DON:	You don't say.

TONY: *(Writhing, grimacing.)* Look –

DEREK: He was only forty. No age at all.

          I can picture him now on his deathbed, saying,

          (In a dying voice.) Never drink whisky, son. You stick to beer.

DON: That what he said?

DEREK: His very last words.

DON: Poor bugger.

DEREK: Tragic.

TONY: *(Writhing, fighting against sickness.)* I'm –

DEREK: Suffered a lot before he died.

DON: Yeah?

DON: Terrible.

DEREK: Don't bear thinking about.

DON: When your liver goes …

TONY: *(Unable to take any more, forcing himself upright into a sitting position.)* FOR FUCKSAKE!

DON: Shush!

DEREK: *(Grinning.)* Alright.

TONY: Look –

DEREK: C'mon. Try to walk.

TONY: *(Groans.)* You're joking.

DEREK: *(Attempts, with DON'S assistance, to raise TONY.)* Just a sprain.

TONY: *(Wriggles free, flops down again on his back.)* No, it's broken.

DON: How d'you know?

TONY: *(Grimaces.)* Can't move it at all.

DEREK: You're not trying.

TONY: *(Whimpering.)* I can't.

DEREK: *(Slightly impatient.)* Oh c'mon.

TONY: *(Groans.)* I feel sick.

DEREK: How much have you had?

DON: *(Very worried.)* Don't throw up in here.

TONY: *(Fighting desperately against sickness.)* My head's spinning like a top.

DON: Just ... take it easy. Think of you mother. Your sister. Your brother.

Your father. Your nephew. *(Panicking, thrusts right hand palm before TONY'S face.)* Stare hard at my hand.

TONY: *(Staring at TONY'S hand.)* What good will *that* do?

DEREK: *(Although clearly also baffled.)* Just do it.

DON: Keep staring.

DEREK: Take deep breaths.

TONY: *(Groans.)* Oh no ...

DEREK: Count to fifty.

TONY: *(Groans loudly.)* Oh my head ...

DON: *(Abandons 'hand routine'.)* Close your eyes.

DEREK: Try to sleep.

DON: You'll soon feel better.

DEREK: Have a good kip.

DON: We'll wake you up in the morning about eight. In time for breakfast.

See how you feel then. If your ankle's no better, take a day off work.

Pay your doctor a visit. I'll take you in the van.

DEREK: But for Godsake, Tony –

DON:	No matter how rough you feel, don't throw up in here.
DEREK:	Try and get to the bog.
DON:	If you can't –
DEREK:	*(Glances at window.)* Through the window.
DON:	*(Glances at window.)* That's your best bet.
DEREK:	It's open.

(Pause.)

Okay?

(Pause.)

Okay Tony?

(Long Pause.)

(Sudden snoring from TONY.)

(To DON.) He's away already.

DON:	*(Sigh of relief.)* Think he'll be alright?
DEREK:	Until he wakes up.
DON:	*(Chuckles.)* He'll be alright, *then.* Silly sod.
DEREK:	*(Yawns.)* Oh well … time we were away.
DON:	Good idea. High time.

I'm ready for a kip.

DEREK:	I'm bloody knackered.

I'll sleep like a log. Been a long day.

DON:	*(Turning towards door.)* Too close. Too dry.

(The door is suddenly kicked wide open.

DIXON stands in the doorway, brandishing a poker.

He is wearing pyjamas, dressing gown and slippers.)

DIXON:	Out.
DON:	*(Reasonably.)* Now, listen –
DIXON:	*(Moves towards them.)* Out!

DON:	L-Look ...
DIXON:	I'm sick to the back teeth. Bloody sick and vomit.
	Every night it's the same stinking story.
	Ranting and raving. Waking every bugger up.
DON:	We –
DIXON:	Waking all the street up. Night after night. Week after week.
DON:	We were only –
DIXON:	I want the pair of you out straight after breakfast.
DON:	Look –
DIXON:	You can both pack your bags first thing in the morning.
DEREK:	*(To DIXON.)* You can't just –
DON:	Derek ...
DIXON:	I want you out after breakfast!
DEREK:	You owe us a week's notice.
DIXON:	*(Moving towards DEREK, who backs away around settee.)*
	You threatening me sonny?
DON:	*(Worriedly.)* Now, look, Mr Dixon –
DIXON:	*(Circling around settee after DEREK.)* Do I hear you threatening me?
DON:	Alright. We'll move out, then.
DEREK:	*(To DON.)* Like hell we will.
DON:	Derek ...
DEREK:	*(Still circling away from DIXON.)* He owes us a week.
	Paid a week in advance. He can't just kick us out.
DIXON:	Oh can't I?
DON:	Listen, Mr Dixon –

DIXON:	*(Stands.)* Pigs! That's all you are! Pigs!
	You're not fit to live in a place like this.
	You're not fit to live anywhere decent at all.
	You can go find a pigsty. That's all you're fit for.
	Go find a pigsty. Stew in your own shit.
DEREK:	*(Angry.)* Now *listen* –
DIXON:	It's the same old story. I take you in out of the goodness of my heart.
	Give you good food. Immaculate rooms. Every facility for a lousy few quid a week and how do you repay me? How do you repay me?
	(Turns on DON.)
	Last week you threw up all over my front garden.
DON:	I'm –
DIXON:	*(Points to DEREK.)* This bugger goes and pisses the bed!
DEREK:	It rains in. The ceiling leaks.
DIXON:	*(To DON.)* The ceiling leaks, he says.
DEREK:	It's *full* of cracks.
DIXON:	*(To DEREK.)* Think I'm *so* green, sonny?
DEREK:	Rains through.
DIXON:	Codswallop! Get to your rooms!
	(Louder.) Go on, get to your rooms!
DEREK:	*(Threateningly, points finger, takes step towards DIXON.)* Look –
DON:	*(Gently pulls DEREK away from DIXON.)* C'mon. C'mon, Derek.
	Let's get some kip.
	(DON lead DEREK, slowly, off.

They exit without taking their eyes off DIXON, who follows, shouting after them from the doorway.)

DIXON: After breakfast do you hear?

(Raises poker, as BRENDA appears, doorway, wearing a nightdress.)

I want you out aft ... *(Breaks off.)*

(Silence.

The poker droops in DIXON'S hand. He backs into the room.

BRENDA follows him, closely, arms akimbo, face angry.)

DIXON: *(Timid.)* I couldn't get to sleep. They were making too much noise.

BRENDA: That was nothing compared to the noise you were making.

Shouldn't be surprised if you've woke all the street up.

What was it all about anyway? Can't you handle them quietly without screaming and shouting?

DIXON: They –

BRENDA: *(Alarmed, points to poker.)* And what's the poker for?

DIXON: It's –

BRENDA: What are you doing?

DIXON: I just –

BRENDA: What are you doing wandering around with *that*?

DIXON: I –

BRENDA: *(Sharp.)* What *are* you doing?

DIXON: I j-just thought I'd scare them.

BRENDA: *(Nods.)* Just thought you'd scare them? For Godsake George!

DIXON: They were making such a racket.

I didn't think you'd mind if –

BRENDA: *(Livid.)* I *do* mind! I bloody well *do!*

DIXON: Calm down.

BRENDA: *(Advancing towards DIXON who backs away around settee.)*

I mind very much, I'll have you know.

I'll have you know I mind very much indeed.

I mind very much, you stupid sod! What the *hell* are you playing at?

Do you want *another* corpse? Are you going round the bend altogether?

DIXON: *(Whimpers, still backing away.)* I didn't mean –

BRENDA: *(Barks angrily.)* Give it to me.

DIXON: I didn't –

BRENDA: *(Louder, snatches poker.)* Give it to me.

DIXON: *(Exits, backing through doorway.)* L-Look –

BRENDA: *(Following him.)* Get out! Go on! Get back to bed!

(She exits.

Long Silence.

TONY begins to snore, loudly.

The light fades, gradually, leaving the room dim, shadowy.

BRENDA suddenly appears, doorway, holding a folded blanket.

She stands a moment, staring at TONY.

She tiptoes tree steps towards TONY, stops as he begins to roll about, restlessly.

She stands, watching, fiddling with the blanket, as TONY begins to cough and groan.

She takes one step forward, stops abruptly, then walks decidedly around to the front of the settee.)

BRENDA: *(Softly, covering TONY with blanket.)* Here, put this over you.

TONY: *(Waking, startled.)* Wha ...!

BRENDA: You'll catch a death of cold. You'll catch a death of cold for yourself, sleeping in here.

TONY: I –

BRENDA: What you been up to? Been drinking again?

TONY: It's my birthday.

BRENDA: Your birthday?

TONY: My twenty-first.

BRENDA: Getaway.

TONY: Yeah.

BRENDA: *(Smiles.)* So you went and got sloshed.

Well, you're only young once.

TONY: *(Winces.)* Nearly broke my bloody neck on the stairs.

BRENDA: *(Giggles.)* Oh so *that's* what it was. Nearly woke all the street.

TONY: I'm sorry. Okay? I'm sorry, I ... *(Groans.)* Think I've broke my right ankle.

BRENDA: *(Swiftly removing TONY'S shoe.)* Let's have a look.

TONY: *(Alarmed.)* Go easy, now.

BRENDA: Don't be soft.

(Pause. BRENDA examines TONY'S ankle.)

No, you've only sprained it.

TONY: How do you know?

BRENDA: If it was broke you'd be in agony.

TONY: I *am* in agony

BRENDA:	Getaway with you.
TONY:	I *am*.
BRENDA:	You're all the same.
TONY:	Eh?
BRENDA:	Men are all the same.
TONY:	How do you mean?
BRENDA:	Least thing and your dying.
TONY:	I feel pain more than most people.
BRENDA:	What makes you think *that?*
TONY:	I just *do*.
BRENDA:	Strange. Once went out with a fella ... used to say the same thing.
	You resemble him, slightly. Same features. Same eyes.
	Same build as well ... he was about your build ... used to sport a moustache ...
TONY:	*(Sits upright, pulls away blanket.)* Like mine?
BRENDA:	No, bushier.
TONY:	Bushier?
BRENDA:	Y'know ... like a Jimmy Edwards?
TONY:	*(Stroking moustache.)* Curling up at each end?
BRENDA:	*(Grimaces.)* That's what put me off him.
	(Sits on settee arm.) Used to drink like a fish.
	Like kissing a wet lettuce.
TONY:	Yeah?
BRENDA:	Yuk.
TONY:	I thought women liked moustaches.
BRENDA:	Oh *some* are alright.
TONY:	*(Strokes moustache.)* Like mine?

BRENDA: Mmn. Suits you. Makes you look distinguished.

TONY: Thought of shaving it off ...

BRENDA: No, keep it on.

TONY: Think I should?

BRENDA: *(Nods.)* It suits you.

TONY: Ah, it's too much trouble ... Think it makes me look older?

BRENDA: *(After considering.)* A bit. Not much.

TONY : Just a bit?

BRENDA: I'd say a year.

TONY: *(Disappointed.)* What? Only a year?

BRENDA: *(Baffled.)* Why do you want to look older?

(Pause.)

TONY: *(Tongue in cheek.)* I prefer older women.

BRENDA: *(Grins.)* That so?

TONY: Every time. They're not as possessive.

Don't demand as much fussing.

BRENDA: Really?

TONY: They're more considerate. More appreciative ... they know the score.

BRENDA: *(Grins.)* Quite a lad, aren't you? Still a chance for me, then?

TONY: Never know you're luck. *(Pointedly.)* You never know your luck.

(Pause.)

(They stare at each other.

BRENDA giggles girlishly.)

BRENDA: I wish I was twenty-one again .

Best time of your life and no mistake.

	(Giggles.) Quite the Belle Of The Ball I was at twenty-one.
TONY:	Bet you never went short.
BRENDA:	*(Quite sharp.)* Never went short?
TONY:	Of ... admirers.
BRENDA:	*(Giggles girlishly.)* Oh I don't know ...
TONY:	Bet you did alright.
BRENDA:	*(Rather bashfully.)* Well, I had my moments.
TONY:	*(Tongue in cheek.)* Different bloke every week?
BRENDA:	Getaway.
TONY:	Bet you had.
BRENDA:	No, I wasn't like that. I was always ... very quiet.

Very quiet ... a bit on the shy side.

(Pause.)

I didn't really go about with many fellas. Just a few. Not many.

Just the odd one ... then I met George.

(Pause.)

He was different then. Altogether different. I Suppose I was too.

Much younger. Stands to reason.

(Pause.)

Every Sunday ... after church ... long walks ... used to go for long walks in the country. Stayed out many an afternoon ... just walking ... laughing ... mile after mile ... just walking ... getting lost.

(Pause.)

Got lost once and finished up in a barn.

It started to rain so we sheltered in a barn.

(Pause.)

He proposed to me there ... in a barn of all places.

(She wipes her eyes.)

He proposed to me there ... in that smelly old barn.

(Pause.)

You're only young once. Just once, that's all.

(She wipes her eyes.)

Before you can turn you're middle-aged ... or old.

(She begins to sob, quietly.

TONY tenderly caresses her hair and shoulders.)

TONY: *(Softly.)* You're not old. Far from it.

BRENDA: *(Between sobs.)* I feel old.

TONY: *(Urgently, turns her face towards him.)* You're *not*.

(Pause.)

(He kisses her, slowly.)

(Softly.) C'mon.

BRENDA: *(Softly.)* Getaway with you.

TONY: C'mon. *(Pulling her slowly down.)* For my birthday.

BRENDA: Sure you feel up to it ... after all this drinking?

TONY: *(Hoarse.)* C'mon.

BRENDA: *(Lying on top of TONY.)* You're a wicked lad.

(They kiss.)

Taking advantage ...

(They kiss passionately.

Blackout. Lights up to dim.

DEREK stands by the door. TONY sleeps.

BRENDA gets up, quietly, from the settee.

She stands a moment, covers TONY with the blanket, gently kisses his forehead, turns to go out.

She is shocked to see DEREK. They stare at each other.)

DEREK: Don't worry. My lips *can* be sealed.

(Blackout.

Lights Up.

Morning.

DON and DEREK are sitting at the table, eating cornflakes, drinking tea.

DEREK reads a newspaper.

TONY lies on the settee, covered by the blanket.

Silence.)

DON: *(Glancing at TONY.)* Better wake him up.

DEREK: Uh?

DON: Tony.

DEREK: What?

DON: Better wake him.

DEREK: *(Glances at TONY.)* Poor bugger.

DON: He won't thank us.

DEREK: Sooner you than me.

DON: *(Irritated.)* Me? Why me? You're his room mate.

DEREK: *(Irritated.)* Alright. I'll wake him, then.

(He continues reading newspaper.

Silence.)

DON: *(Staring at TONY.)* At least he's not been sick.

(Pause.)

A miracle in itself.

(Pause.)

Thank God he's not.

Thank God for that.

(Pause.)

Bet he knows about it.

(Pause.)

Bloody clown.

(Pause.)

Bet he knows about it.

(Pause.)

When he wakes.

(Pause.)

Feel like Noddy in hell.

(Pause.)

Head bigger than Birkenhead.

(Pause.)

(Sighs, shakes head.) Silly bastard.

(Pause.)

Don't envy him that.

(DIXON storms in, carrying two plates of eggs and bacon.

He slams the plates down before DON and DEREK, then storms out again without looking at either of them.

DON and DEREK stare briefly at each other.

DON shrugs his shoulders, stares back at TONY.

DEREK shakes head, continues reading.

Silence.)

DON: Better wake him up.

(Pause.)

Before smiler comes back with his breakfast.

(Pause.)

Better wake him up now.

(Pause.)

DEREK: *(Looks at DON.)* What d'you reckon?

DON: Eh?

DEREK: Reckon he means it?

DON: Who?

DEREK: Dixon?

DON: Nah , he's all talk. Bark's worse than his bite.

Look, for Godsake wake Tony up before he comes back.

(DEREK sighs, rises.

(DIXON storms in, carrying a bowl of cornflakes and a plate of eggs and bacon.

He slams them down on the table.)

DON: Look, we're sorry.

DIXON: One more chance. Just one more chance.

I'll give you both one more chance, then next time ... *(Points to door.)* out.

I'm just not prepared to keep on putting up with it.

The missus ain't either. We've both had enough.

DON: We –

DIXON: Night after night it's always the same.

I've told you 'til I'm blue in the face this lounge is closed after half-past ten. Just step out of line once more, that's all.

Just step out of line once more and you're *(Points to door.)* out.

DON: We didn't realise we were making so much noise. We're sorry.

DIXON: Complaints galore from the neighbours, I'm getting.

Every day without fail. Complaints galore. All I ask is a bit of peace and quiet. Not a lot to ask, is it? I'm a reasonable man.

Just a bit of peace and quiet. That's all I ask. And what do I get?

(Throws his arms in the air) Complaints galore.

DON: It won't happen again.

DIXON: Every week's the same.

DON: Look –

DIXON: Always trouble. Bloody endless trouble.

Here, why do I put up with you?

(DEREK moves to TONY, begins to shake him, gently.)

Be buggered if I know. Why *do* I put up with you?

Can you answer me that?

DON: Well –

DIXON: It's laughable, really. It really is laughable.

Here I am farting around like this. A man of my experience.

Thirty years in the force. Pissballing around.

Waiting on you hand and foot. When there's no need to do it!

No need at all! I could live off my pension. Do a few gardens.

Plenty gardens around here. Make a wage up easily.

Everybody *hates* gardening. Around here, anyway.

No bugger can be bothered. Too much trouble.

Sooner sit on their fat arses, gawping at the box.

(Pause.)

I could make a good wage. I'm a qualified gardener.

(Pause.)

But instead I'm farting round waiting hand and foot on a bunch of … *(Breaks off, groans.)* Well, anyway come summer, I'm selling this place.

(To DEREK, points to TONY.) What's wrong with him?

DEREK:	*(Shakes TONY.)* Dunno. Can't wake him.
DIXON:	*(To DON.)* He slept there all night?
DON:	*(Feebly.)* Don't think so. No.
DIXON:	Getting more like a doss house every stinking day.
DEREK:	*(Shakes TONY, vigorously.)* Tony. C'mon.
DON:	Try slapping his face.
DEREK:	*(Slaps TONY'S face.)* Tony. C'mon. Wake up.
DIXON:	*(Wearily.)* Stroll on.
	(DON rises, moves to TONY.)
DON:	*(Slaps TONY'S face.)* Tony. Wake up, boy.
DIXON:	What a bloody shower.
DEREK:	*(To DON.)* He's not breathing.
DON:	'Course he is.
DEREK:	He's stone cold.
DON:	*(Listening for TONY'S heartbeat.)* He's still breathing.
DEREK:	Sure?
	(Pause.)
DON:	*(Nods.)* He's still breathing.
DEREK:	*(Listening for TONY'S heartbeat.)* I can't hear him.
DON:	His ticker's still going.

DEREK:	He's out like a light.
DON:	*(Shakes TONY, vigorously.)* Tony. C'mon boy. Wake up. Rise and shine.
DEREK:	Rise and shine, Tony.
DON:	Breakfast is out.
DEREK:	*(Shakes TONY'S legs.)* Nice crispy bacon.
DON:	*(Shakes TONY'S shoulders.)* Two eggs.
DEREK:	One sausage.
DON:	Cornflakes.
DEREK:	Toast and tea.
DON:	*Marmalade* toast. *(Shakes TONY.)* C'mon. Wake up.
DIXON:	*(Barks, moves across to them.)* What the hell's wrong with him?
DEREK:	*(To DIXON, as DON feels TONY'S pulse.)* He's finished.
DIXON:	He's ... what?
DEREK:	He's dead.
DON:	*(Looks up, slowly.)* Looks like it.
DEREK:	He's snuffed it.
DIXON:	Bloody hell! *(He shakes TONY, violently.)* C'mon! Rise and shine! D'you hear me?! Wake up!
DON:	It's no use.
DEREK:	He's had it.
DON:	Poor sod.
DEREK:	Kicked the bucket.
DON:	Alcoholic poisoning.
DEREK:	That's what's done it. No doubt about it. Drink's to blame.

DIXON: *(Shakes TONY, violently.)* Wake up! D'you hear me?!

DEREK: *(To DIXON.)* You're wasting your time.

DON: *(To DIXON.)* He can't hear you.

DEREK: He's dead.

DIXON: *(Slaps TONY'S face, feels his pulse.)* Wake up!

(Silence.

All three stare at TONY.

DIXON shakes head, groans, releases TONY, flops down into the armchair.

Throughout the following dialogue he stares straight ahead.

His remarks go unheard by DON and DEREK who talk to each other, staring at TONY.)

DIXON: Stroll on.

DON: Tragic.

DIXON: This is *all* I need.

DON: Couldn't meet a nicer bloke.

DEREK: First class room-mate.

DON: Bloody tragic.

DEREK: One of the best.

DON: Life's very short.

DIXON: Always trouble.

DON: Have to tell his parents.

DEREK: No need. They're both dead. A car crash.

DON: Oh.

(Pause.)

Ah well …

DEREK: Terrible.

DON:	Comes to us all.
DEREK:	Too true.
DON:	Inevitable.
DIXON:	Couldn't have picked a worse time.
	People coming for tea ...
DON:	Has he any relatives?
DEREK:	Never mentioned any.
DON:	If there are, they'll have to be notified.
DEREK:	Right.
DIXON:	*(Bitterly.)* Owed me three weeks rent!
DON:	I still can't believe it.
DEREK:	What?
DON:	That he's dead.
DEREK:	Takes a while to sink in.
	(Pause.)
	First corpse I've seen.
DON:	*(Mildly surprised.)* Really?
DEREK:	Yeah.
DON:	First one?
DEREK:	Straight up.
DON:	First ever?
DEREK:	Umn.
	(Pause.)
DON:	You're taking it well.
DEREK:	Think so?
DON:	Considering ...
DEREK:	How d'you mean?
DON:	*(Shrugs.)* Well, you're not exactly shitting yourself.

DEREK:	Should I be?
DON:	I did. First corpse I saw.
DEREK:	Straight up?
DON:	You bet I did.
DEREK:	Shit yourself?
DON:	Seven shades of green.
DEREK:	*(Shrugs.)* Affects people differently.
DON:	Bear in mind, though … *(Breaks off.)*
DEREK:	What?
DON:	See … she made a weird noise.
DEREK:	Eh?
DON:	My first corpse. My gran.
	(Pause.)
DEREK:	*Made a weird noise?*
DON:	That's what *really* got me. That's what *made* me shit myself.
DEREK:	How old were you?
DON:	Six.
DEREK:	Six?
DON:	Nearly seven.
DEREK:	Oh *well* …
DON:	That's what did it. I mean, if she'd remained silent.
	Silent as the grave, she wouldn't have affected me that way at all. I've seen plenty of corpses since and *they* haven't affected me. Well, they've not *frightened* me, anyway.
	It was the noise she made.
	(Pause.)
DEREK:	She *was* dead, wasn't she?

DON: Dead as a doornail.

DEREK: Then how could she …?

DON: Dunno. But she did.

(Pause.)

DEREK: What sort of noise was it?

DON: Weird. Bloody weird. See, she used to live with us.

My granny, she lived with us. When she died she lay in state for a day in our back bedroom.

(Pause.)

I remember … pestering my mother something awful to let me see her before they carted her away.

I gave her no peace and finally she did.

She took me upstairs to where gran was lying.

(Pause.)

We just sort of … stared at her.

She looked so … contented.

She was actually smiling. Well, not smiling … leering.

She never really smiled. It was more of a leer.

She just lay there … leering back at us. Strange.

Her eyes were half open. She looked much younger.

Seemed chuffed with herself. Seemed tickled pink.

It was almost as if … she'd finally won.

(Pause.)

She looked … distinctly tickled.

(Pause.)

After a while my mother went out.

Went out to the toilet. Left me alone.

(Pause.)

I kept on staring ... down at her.

(Pause.)

I was really fascinated.

(Pause.)

First corpse I'd seen.

(Pause.)

Remember, I was only six.

(Pause.)

Then ... I kissed her ... whilst my mother was out.

DEREK: You kissed her?

DON: I liked her. She'd been good to me. Always buying me toys.

So I kissed her goodbye and that's when it happened ...

DEREK: As you kissed her?

DON: She sort of ... belched in my ear.

(Pause.)

DEREK: Belched?

DON: Straight up.

DEREK: But how could she ...?

DON: Locked wind escaping.

DEREK: Locked wind?

DON: *(Shrugs.)* That's what my old man put it down to.

DEREK: *(Incredulous.)* Locked wind?

DON: He said the same thing had happened to him
except his old granny had farted instead.

DEREK: *(Grimaces.)* Yuk.

DON: Put him *right* off his beer for a week.

DEREK: No wonder.

DON: Terrible.

DEREK: Give *anyone* the shits.

            (Pause.)

DIXON: *(Wearily, to DON.)* What have I done to deserve all this?

            Can you tell me? I mean, I must have done something.

            Not the first time it's happened. People dropping dead.

            It's been one a year for the past five years. I must have done something. Last year it was Tom.

DON: *(To DIXON.)* He was old.

DIXON: Old my arse. He was only fifty- one.

DEREK: *(To DON.)* What did *he* die of?

DON: Had a heart attack.

DEREK: Oh.

DON: Died on the toilet. Had to break the door down.

DIXON: *(Rises, irritated.)* Cost an arm and a leg for a new bloody door!

            Always finish up forking out. Joe Soap, that's me.

            People dropping dead all over the place. It's a regular habit.

            They come here to die. Come here to snuff it. Regular stint.

            Every year without fail.

            (As BRENDA enters, wearing a demure dress, carrying a large pot of tea.)

DIXON: Fucking roll on.

            (BRENDA stops abruptly, clears her throat, loudly.

All three turn, stare at her.

She stares at DIXON.)

DIXON: Brenda ...

BRENDA: *(Placing teapot on table.)* Well, George ... delightful language first thing in the morning.

DIXON: *(Points to TONY.)* This lad, Tony, he's ...

BRENDA: Delightful language.

DIXON: This lad, Tony, he's ...

(Pause.)

BRENDA: *(Stares at TONY.)* What's wrong with him?

(Pause.)

What's wrong with him?

(Pause.)

DIXON: *(Softly.)* He's dead.

(Pause.)

BRENDA: *(Softly.)* Dead?

DON: Afraid so.

DIXON: Too much drink.

BRENDA: *(Softly, totters slightly, grips edge of table.)* Oh God ...

DIXON: *(Moves to her, with DON.)* Steady on.

DEREK: *(Points to armchair.)* Look, sit her down here.

(DON and DIXON help BRENDA into the armchair.

She begins to sob, very quietly.

DIXON sits on chair arm, his arm around her.

She continues sobbing.

DON and DEREK watch.)

DIXON: *(Gently, to BRENDA.)* I know it's a shock. So sudden. I know ...

	Why don't you just go and have a lie down?
	Lie down on the bed and I'll bring you some tea?
BRENDA:	*(Wipes eyes.)* Such a shock ...
DIXON:	I know.
BRENDA:	*(Sobs afresh.)* So young.
	(Pause.)
DEREK:	*(Softly.)* Took it bad.
DON:	Big shock.
DEREK:	Affects women more.
DON:	Seems to. Yeah.
	(Pause.)
	(They turn, stare at TONY.
	BRENDA sobs, very quietly, throughout the following.)
DON:	*(Covering TONY'S face with blanket.)* He *was* on about his heart.
DEREK:	Oh yeah.
DON:	Uh. Such a waste. What a waste.
	(Pause.)
	Such a great bloody waste.
	(Pause.)
	Must have drunk *a lot*. Though he didn't seem *so* bad.
	(Turns to DEREK.) Last night. He didn't seem all that bad.
DEREK:	No.
DON:	Still ...
DEREK:	*(With some conviction.)* Must have died peacefully in his sleep.
	No pain. Best way to go. Well ... one of the best.

DON:	It *is* the best.
DEREK:	No, I wouldn't say that.
DON:	What's the best way, then?
DEREK:	On the job.
DON:	Oh yeah.
DEREK:	*On the job.*
DON:	Yeah, I think you're right.
DEREK:	Take some beating. Think of it.
	(Closes eyes, dreamily.) What a way to go.
	(Pause.)
DON:	What *was* his job?
DEREK:	A menswear salesman.
DON:	*(Mildly surprised.)* Really?
DEREK:	On Oxford Street.
DON:	Selling, like?
DEREK:	A salesman. Yeah.
	(Pause.)
	Got some smart shirts.
DON:	I noticed.
DEREK:	And suits. Talk about suits ... his wardrobe's full of em.
DON:	I'll bet it is, too.
DEREK:	Has three wardrobes.
DON:	*Three?*
DEREK:	Couldn't manage with one. Has too many suits Bought two portable wardrobes only last week.
DON:	How many suits has he?
DEREK:	*(After considering.)* Must have forty at least.
DON:	*(Astounded.)* Forty?

DEREK:	All brand new.
DON:	Forty suits?
DEREK:	Never been worn.
DON:	More money than sense.
DEREK:	He was after his own set-up.
DON:	Oh, I see ...
DEREK:	That was his ambition.

(Pause.)

(Strokes chin, thoughtfully.) There's some money in rags if you find the right location. Fashion's the thing, now. No doubt about that.

In London, especially. You can't go wrong, man.

DON:	What about all the overheads? You need a few grand.
DEREK:	No, not necessarily.
DON:	How d'you mean?
DEREK:	Look, what he was after ... what Tony was after was a stall ... a stall on Petticoat Lane.
DON:	A stall?
DEREK:	To start off with. Just as a start.

The suits are all sizes. Shirts as well.

He must have a stock of sixty shirts, at least.

DON:	Sixty shirts?
DEREK:	Inside cases on top of his wardrobes.

He was after flogging it all down the lane.

DON:	But where'd he get the money to buy all this stuff?
DEREK:	*Oh come on.* That's none of our business.

(Pause. They stare at TONY.)

BRENDA:	*(To DIXON, wiping eyes.)* Have you phoned the doctor?

DIXON: Our phone's not working.

BRENDA: Again?

DIXON: They've not been to fix it.

BRENDA: Tut. Have to go down the road, then.

DIXON: I'll go in a minute.

BRENDA: So young.

DIXON: *(Gently, pulls her closer to him.)* C'mon.

BRENDA: Twenty-one.

            (She stares ahead. Dixon strokes her head, gently.)

DEREK: *(Thoughtfully, to DON.)* Not a bad idea, is it?

DON: Eh?

DEREK: Getting a stall?

DON: No.

DEREK: Not a bad idea.

DON: Had his head screwed on.

DEREK: No flies on Tony.

DIXON: *(Softly, to BRENDA.)* I'll ring Albert and Doreen as well.

            Tell them they can come next week instead.

            I'll explain the position. They'll understand.

            (Pats her shoulder, gently.) C'mon, dry your eyes.

DEREK: I was down there last week. Petticoat Lane. Sunday morning.

            Packed. Absolutely choco-block.

DON: Always is.

DEREK: Not a bad idea, getting a stall …

DON: *(Strokes chin, thoughtfully.)* Thought about it, myself.

            Independence …

DEREK:	Your own governor. That's *gotta* be better. No doubt about that.
DON:	*(Glancing at watch.)* Shit. It's half-past eight.
DEREK:	Never.
DON:	*(Shows watch to DEREK.)* It is, y'know.
DEREK:	*(Wearily.)* Bloody late again.
DON:	They'll be giving *me* the bullet. Every morning ... how's your job going?
DEREK:	Stinks. Really giving me the hump. It's a mug's game working for somebody else. Waste of time altogether.
	No incentive. None at all. You slave your balls off lining their pockets. What's the point? They're never satisfied.
	You're no better thought of. The more you do ... reach sixty-five, you've nothing to show.
DON:	Get given a crappy clock.
DEREK:	Or a kick up the arse.
	(They chuckle ironically. DEREK leans on the settee. *DON stands. They stare down at TONY.* *Pause.* *Sudden thunder heard, briefly, outside.)*
DIXON:	*(Softly.)* Hello, it's thundering, now. It's perhaps as well.
	Perhaps as well Albert and Doreen won't be coming.
	I shouldn't think they'd fancy it. Thunder and rain. *(Pause.)*
	It's perhaps as well. *(Pause.)*
DEREK:	*(Quietly.)* Look, what do you say we ...?

(He breaks off, nods slowly towards TONY.)

DON: *(Nods slowly towards TONY.)* You mean …? *(Breaks off.)*

DEREK: *(Stands upright.)* I'm game.

DON: Down the lane?

DEREK: Where else? We'll need your van. Go halves on petrol.

I know a guy there who'll help find us a pitch.

DON: I dunno …

DEREK: *(Quietly, with conviction.)* It's *got* to be worth a go, Don.

Did you read about that bloke in the paper last week?

DON: Who was that?

DEREK: Whatsisname … Anyway, well, this bloke set up in business six years ago with one little stall in Portabello Road.

One stall. Now he owns fourteens shops, a restaurant and a mansion in the south of France.

DON: Goes to show …

DEREK: Six years. *We can do the same.* There's nothing to stop us.

I have a few contacts. We're halfway there, man.

We've nothing to lose.

DON: *(Hesitant.)* I dunno …

DEREK: What's the problem?

DON: *(Shrugs.)* Just seems a bit … well …I just think it might play on my conscience, that's all.

DEREK: Oh c'mon. For Godsake. Look, let's be realistic.

(With conviction.) After all's said and done, we'll only be doing what Tony would want us to do.

DON: How'd you mean?

DEREK: We'll fulfil his ambition. It's the *least* we can do for him.

DON: Well ...

DEREK: What do you say?

DON: *(Shrugs.)* If you look at it like that ...

DEREK: *(Extending hand to DON.)* Fifty-fifty? Fair enough?

(DON hesitates a moment,

shakes DEREK'S hand, slowly.)

Let's go, take a look at the stock.

(They begin to move off.

DEREK exits.

DON stops, stands in the doorway.

He turns, slowly, stares at TONY.)

DEREK'S, voice off: *(Brisk.)* C'mon, then!

(DON turns, goes out, closing the door.

Silence.

More thunder heard, briefly, slightly louder than before.

The light fades, gradually, very slowly, as BRENDA and DIXON talk, softly.)

BRENDA: He was nice.

DIXON: C'mon.

BRENDA: A nice boy.

DIXON: Yes.

BRENDA: Much nicer than the others.

DIXON: Yes.

(Pause.)

BRENDA: It was thundering –

DIXON: Listen ...

BRENDA: – the day you proposed to me.

            (Pause.)

            Remember?

DIXON: Yes.

BRENDA: It was thundering then.

            (Pause.)

DIXON: How long is it? Nineteen?

BRENDA: Twenty next month.

            (Pause.)

DIXON: It's thundered a lot since then.

BRENDA: Yes.

            (Pause.)

DIXON: Things *will* be better ... between us ... yes?

            (Pause.)

            I promise things *will* ... be better.

            (Pause.)

            I *will* ... see someone. I'll do as you said. I *do* ... still love –

BRENDA: *(Softly, stares ahead.)* Love you.

            (Blackout.

            Lights up.

            Morning. TONY's body has been removed.

            DON and DEREK are finishing breakfast.

            They both put down their knives and forks.)

DON: Well, *that* was an improvement. A *big* improvement.

            A *choice* of cereals, would you believe?

            Two eggs, baked beans, and *sausages too!*

Anyone would think we were staying at the Ritz!

DEREK: And there's more to come.

DON: Really? How do you mean?

DEREK: He's bringing us toast and raspberry jam.

DON: *(Amazed.)* Jam?

DEREK: Or marmalade if you prefer.

DON: But *why? Why now?* What I don't understand is why, all of a sudden, things have improved.

One minute, the breakfast wouldn't feed a sparrow and the next we're eating one fit for a King?

DEREK: Like I said, all I did was have a quiet word. A word with Brenda.

DON: Oh, *first names, now.*

DEREK: She agreed with me that standards had slipped.

DON: Just like that?

DEREK: *(Imitates Tommy Cooper.)* Just like that.

DON: But what about Dixon? What about him?

DEREK: He'll do just as he's told.

(DIXON bursts in with toast and jam on a tray.

He slams the tray down on the table.)

DIXON: *(Barks, collecting used plates.)* This is just a one-off.

I hope you realise that.

DEREK: Beg your pardon, Mr Dixon?

DIXON: Just a one-off!

DEREK: I'm not sure I follow ...

DIXON: This breakfast! Today! It won't be repeated!

DEREK: Are you sure about that?

(BRENDA appears, doorway.)

BRENDA: George, why are you shouting? Come along!

Now! We've a sink full of dishes.

DEREK: *(Cheerfully* to *DIXON.)* I think you'd better go.

(BRENDA exits.)

DIXON: *(More meekly.)* Just don't … don't push it.

Don't push it, that's all.

BRENDA'S voice, off: George!

DEREK: *(Smiles, waves gently to DIXON.)* Better go. Toodle pip.

(DIXON, fuming, storms out.

Pause.

Loud *Music. 'Groovin' With Mr Bloe'.*

Blackout.)